MY MOMMY'S SPECIAL

DEDICATION

I can only dedicate this book to one person—
My Special Mommy

Love,

Jennifer

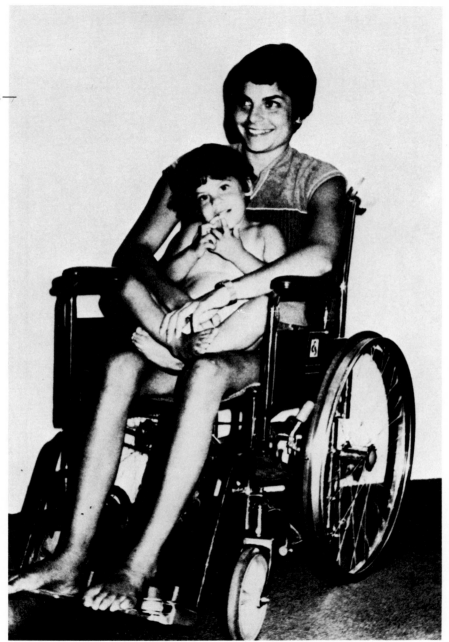

2

MY MOMMY'S SPECIAL

By Jennifer English

CHILDRENS PRESS, CHICAGO®

This book is not a fairy tale, but there is a queen in it. Mostly it's about my mommy and me and when I was little.

Library of Congress Cataloging in Publication Data
English, Jennifer.
  My mommy's special.
  (Real-life photo stories)
  Summary: A little girl describes all the things
she does with her mother who is confined to a wheelchair.
  1. Handicapped parents—Juvenile literature.
2. Mothers and daughters—Juvenile literature.
[1. Mothers and daughters.   2. Physically handicapped]
I. Title.   II. Series.
HQ759.912.E54   1985   306.8'743'0924   85-12836
ISBN 0-516-03861-3

I go to school now, and one day our
teacher said, "We're going to write
stories and make some books." So I
wrote this story about Mommy.

My mommy's not really
different from other
mommies. She just has to
sit in a chair all day. She
cannot run around like
you and me. Her legs are
weak and she can't walk.
So she has to use a
wheelchair.

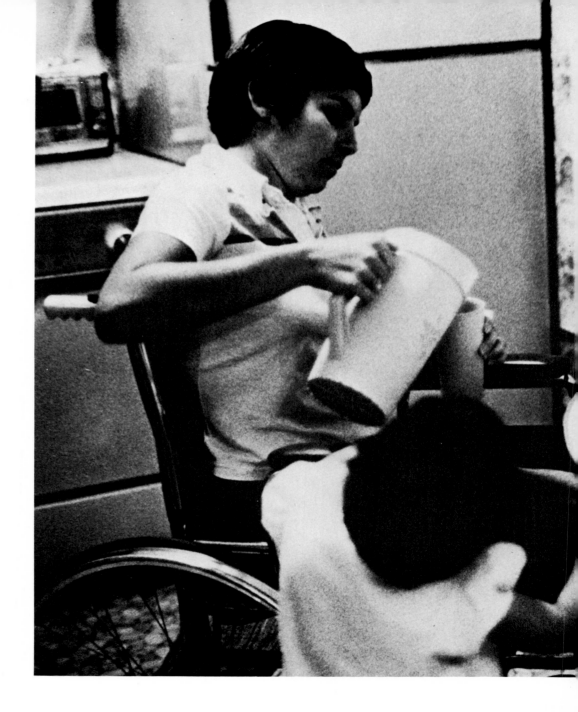

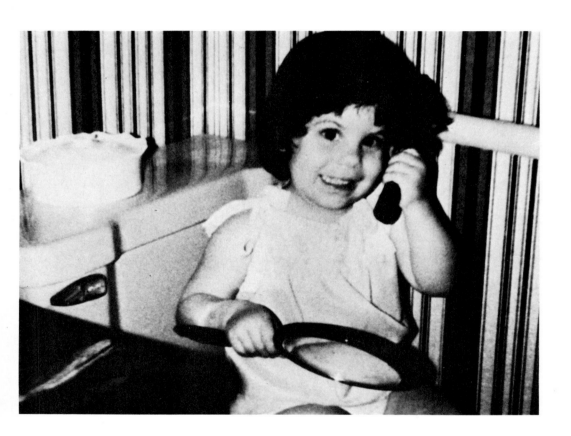

That is why we are a
team. I can do things
Mommy can't do and she
can do things I can't do.
We have been a team
ever since I was little.

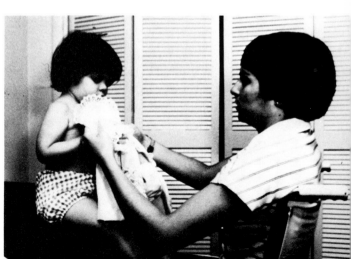

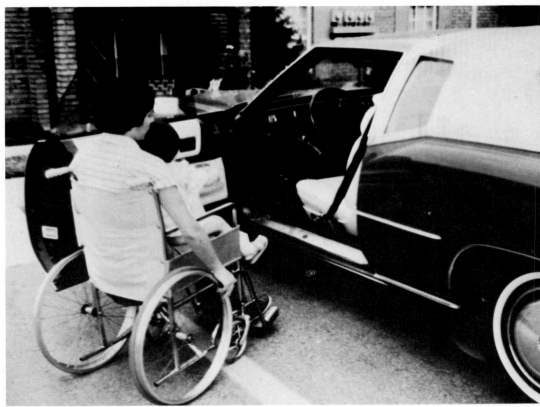

Whenever we went shopping, I would carry the coupons and get the things off the shelves.

Everyone always seemed surprised when we went shopping. I don't know why. We always did it.

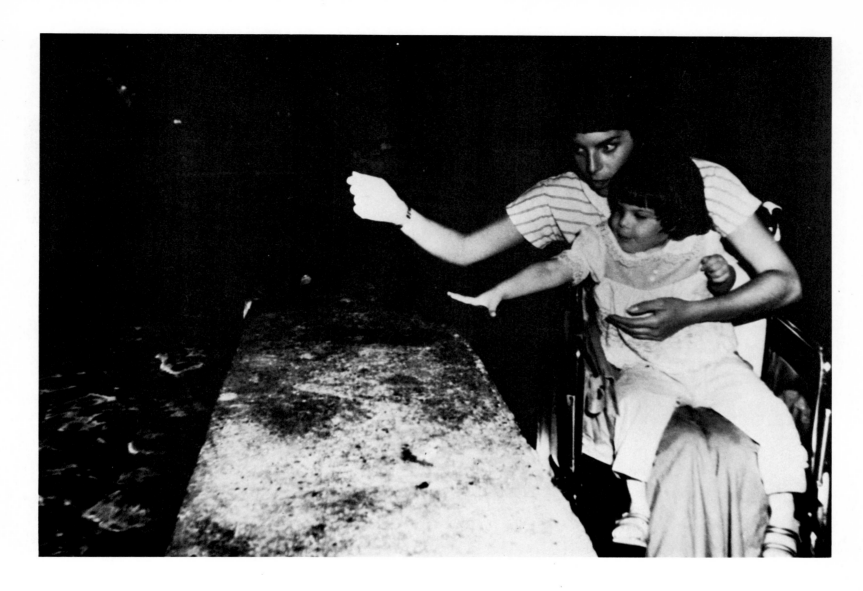

When we finished, we never forgot
to throw a penny into the fountain and
make our wishes.

Sometimes I got to ride the toy train
at the shopping center.

Mommy and I always worked together.

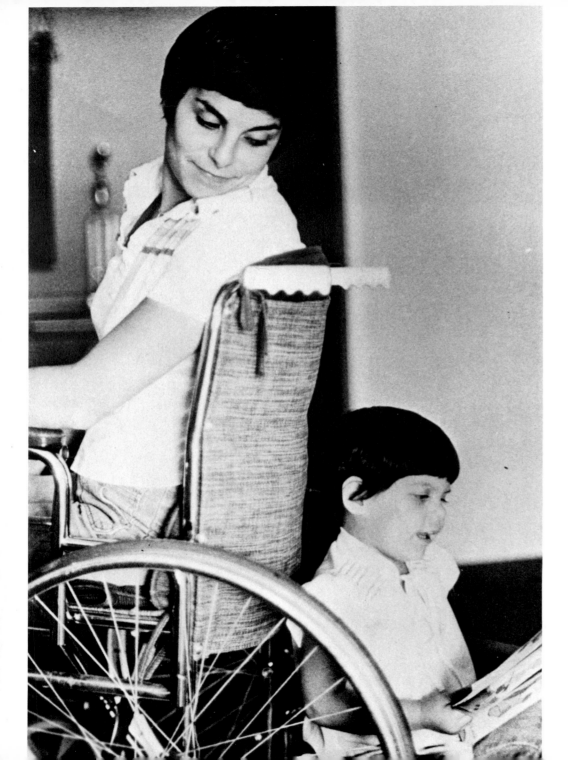

We just took our time doing what we wanted to do—like reading, playing games, lying in the sun, drawing, or just cuddling.

13

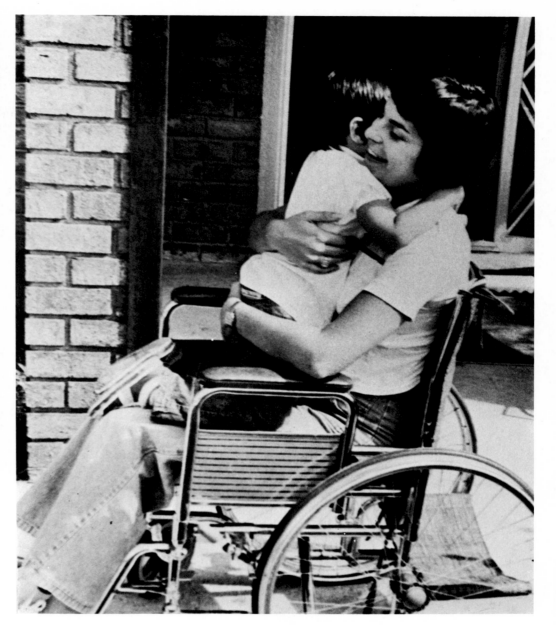

We had secrets, too, that only we knew about.

One year Mommy was crowned Miss Wheelchair Virginia.

16

I got to go with her then.

We were on TV and our pictures
were in the newspapers, too.

She let me wear her
crown sometimes.

Mommy was special to everybody that year.

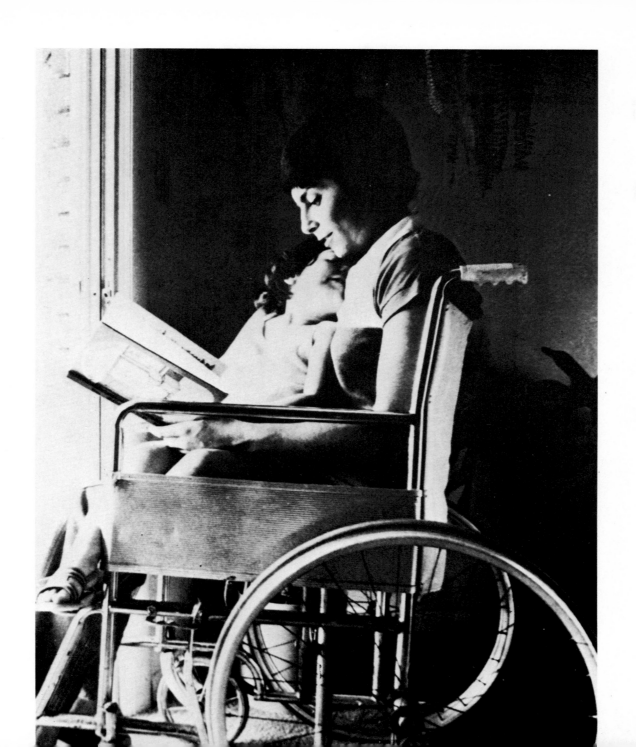

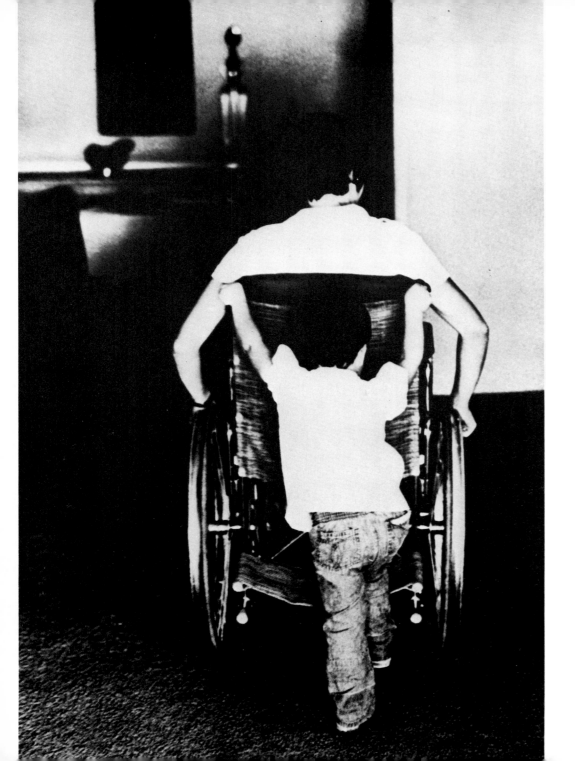

Mommy and I were
always a good team.

24

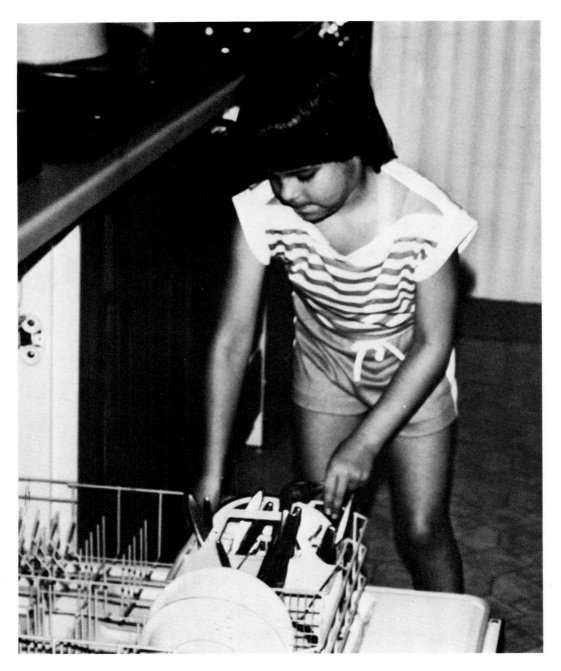

Now that I am bigger
I can do things I couldn't
do before.

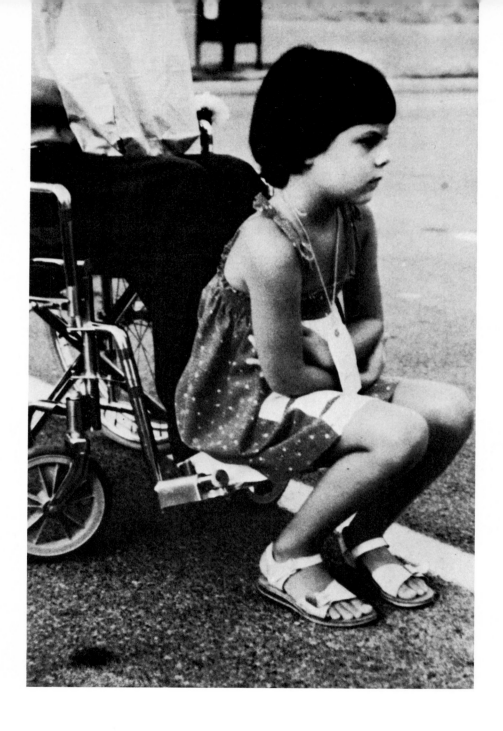

When I started school,
I worried about Mommy.
I thought, "Who will play
with her?" But Mommy
has a friend who comes to
see her every day.

When I come home from school, Mommy always has a surprise for me and my best friend Mandy. Our favorite is popsicles!

Mandy and I have lots of fun jumping
rope or playing with our dolls.

Once we went to the children's zoo.
I even got to pet a billy goat.

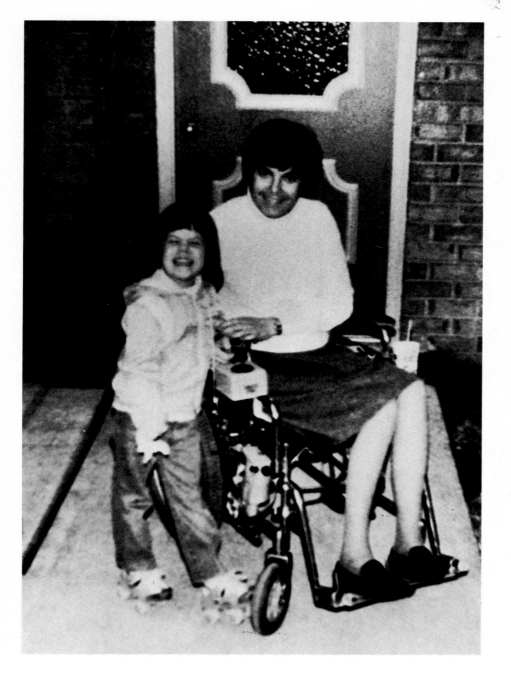

Now you see that my mommy is just like your mommy, except that she has to sit in that chair. The next time you see somebody sitting in a wheelchair, you can think of my mommy and me, and remember that they are not so different after all.

If they are like my mommy, they are very special.

About the Author

I was born on January 4, 1978, in Roanoke, Virginia. Now I live in Salem, Virginia, with my mother and stepfather and my cat, Bonus.

I like to read, write stories, and draw. I also like music and I have studied ballet for three years. At East Salem Elementary School I am a cheerleader, which is a lot of fun.

Mommy says I am a big help to her. She has multiple sclerosis. Bonus tries to help, too, by entertaining Mommy and me.

My hobbies are cooking and photography. I bought my own camera with the money I saved from my allowance and my tooth fairy money.

Here is a picture of me that someone else took.